Growing Into a Family

A Kid's Guide to Living in a Blended Family

Written by
Cynthia Geisen

Illustrated by
R. W. Alley

Publications
St. Meinrad, IN 47577

With thanks to my own sisters, with whom
I have shared the rough and tumble and joy of blending.
And with thanks most of all to Ryan, my next-of-kin.

Published by Abbey Press Publications
1 Hill Drive
St. Meinrad, Indiana 47577

Library of Congress Catalog Number
2015938522

ISBN 978-0-87029-684-0

Printed in the United States of America.

A Message to Parents, Teachers, and Other Caring Adults

The secret to blending families is there is no secret. It's scary and awesome and ragged and perfect and always changing. Love and laugh hard. Try again tomorrow. But that's life advice, right?

—*Mir Kamin*

Families blend together for a variety of reasons. Widowed or divorced parents choose to remarry. An ailing or elderly relative can no longer live alone and moves in with his son's family. A family chooses to adopt a child. Economic circumstances force family members to combine households. Regardless of *why* it happens, creating a blended family is a process of transition that takes time, patience, humor, compassion, and a whole lot of conversation.

Therefore, this book has been designed not so much to be read *by* a child than to be read *with* a child you love. You'll notice that several pages invite you to craft lists of: family traditions, things you like to do together, the things in your child's life that have changed, and those that have stayed the same. "Your child" is not intended to be literal, but to refer to a child you love. Aunts, uncles, teachers, pastors, and friends would be wonderful reading companions.

The purpose is three-fold. First, to give your child permission to talk with you about the things with which she or he may be struggling. Second, to create a structured space so that you are able to listen to and talk with one another. Third, to model for your child a healthy way to deal with the transitions that will certainly come her or his way in the future.

As you approach this book, don't be daunted. There are no magic formulas and no right answers. More than anything, you will be gifting your child with your presence. Just bring your love, compassion, persistence, and a large dollop of humor. May you have each in abundance.

—*Cynthia Geisen*

A Family's Love Never Changes

Your family is important. It's the place where you feel safe and loved. Family members are people you can count on. No matter what happens, your family's love for you will never change. You can count on your family because they want what is best for you. They want you to be happy and always to feel loved.

Who is in your family? Do you have sisters and brothers? Grandparents? Aunts? Uncles? Cousins? Stepbrothers and stepsisters? A stepmom or stepdad?

Isn't it great to think of all the people who love you!

When Families Grow

Sometimes, new members join a family. You may have heard that *your* family is getting ready to grow. It could be that your mom or dad is getting married to someone who has children. Maybe your grandfather is coming to live with you. Or, perhaps your parents are going to adopt a baby from a faraway country.

You might be wondering: How will things in my family change? How will I fit in? Will I still be important?

It's okay to have lots of questions.

It's Okay to Ask

You are probably wondering about lots of things. Where will I live? Do I have to share my room? What will my step-sister or brother be like? Will we get along? What should I call my stepmom or stepdad? Is it okay to talk about my "real" mom or dad? Will we still have chocolate cake on my birthday?

Maybe you have other questions, too.

Talk about your questions with your mom, dad, or another adult you trust. No question is silly or wrong. Asking questions helps us know what to expect. So, don't be afraid to ask!

Many Things Change

Lots of changes are happening in your family. What are they? Do you sleep in a different room? Go to a new school? Do you have new stepbrothers and stepsisters? Maybe you have two homes now, instead of one.

Sit down with an adult you love and make a list of all the new things in your life. Draw a star by all the items on your list that you really like. Put an "X" by the new things in your life that are hard or that you don't like.

Talk together about everything on your list.

Some Things Stay the Same

Even though lots of things are different in your family, some things are still the same. Think of all the things in your life that are the way they have always been. Maybe you still have the same pet. Or, you still might like to play hide-and-seek. It could be that ice cream is still your favorite dessert.

Ask an adult you love to help you make a list of all the things in your life that have *not* changed.

Don't forget to put this on your list: "My family loves me." That will always stay the same.

Everyone Has Feelings

If someone asked, "How are you feeling about the changes in your family?" what would you say? Do you feel: happy…sad…afraid…mad… confused…lonely…excited?

It's normal to have feelings. Everyone has emotions, especially when important things are happening in our lives. You may find that your emotions change often. Or, that people feel differently about the very same thing. For example, you may feel happy when you hold your pet lizard, "Sally." However, your stepdad might not want to touch her.

Share Your Feelings with an Adult You Trust

You probably have many feelings about the changes happening in your family. You might feel excited *and* scared about living in a new house. Or, you may feel mad *and* happy that you are going to have a new brother. It's okay to feel more than one feeling at the same time.

Talk with your dad, mom, or another adult about your feelings. They can help you find ways to understand and express your emotions. For example, you might try hitting a pillow (instead of your brother) when you are mad.

Staying in Touch

Do you have a favorite stuffed animal? Maybe you have a picture of your mom or dad that you like a lot. Sometimes, when many things are changing, it feels good to have something familiar close by. Ask your mom or dad if you can hang a picture on the wall of your room or put something on your desk that makes you feel happy.

Hearing the voice of someone you love is also comforting. Even when you are away from your mom or dad, you can talk on the phone or on the computer and tell them about your day.

Working Together to Smooth Out the Bumps

Have you ever hit a bump? Maybe you were riding your bike or in the car when you felt a big THUMP. Sometimes roads are not as smooth as we would like.

The same is true with families. We may fight with our sisters and brothers. We might say hurtful things. Sometimes, we just have a hard time getting along.

Every family hits bumps now and then. It's part of being a family. But, you can work together to smooth out the bumps. Your parents might call a family meeting so you can talk together about how to make things run more smoothly.

Practice, Practice, Practice

Some things happen all at once, like blowing out birthday candles or getting splashed in a puddle. Other things take a little time, like learning to ride a bike or baking cookies. Getting used to your new routine and learning to live with new family members will not happen all at once. Just like it took time for you to learn your ABCs, it will also take time for you to adjust to the changes in your family.

But, there's good news! Adjusting to your new routine and learning to live with your new family members gets easier with practice.

Have an Adventure

Do you like adventures? Maybe you like to visit the zoo and pretend that you are on a safari. Or, you might enjoy riding roller coasters with lots of twists and turns. When you're having an adventure, you don't always know what's next. Part of the fun is being surprised!

Pretend that you and your family are on an adventure together. Have fun learning about each other. Expect a few surprises!

African Plains

WELCOME!!!

Has anyone ever made you feel welcome? They asked your name. Maybe they offered you a cookie, shared their toys, or invited you to play a game. Even if you didn't know each other before, it soon felt like you had known each other for a long time.

The same thing can happen with new members of your family. You can be welcoming. Invite your stepbrothers and stepsisters to play a game or watch a video with you. Ask your grandma or grandpa to go for a walk.

You may have heard the *Golden Rule*: treat others as you want to be treated.

Family's Traditions: Old and New

What are your family's traditions? Do you make sandcastles on the beach in the summer? Leave cookies out for Santa on Christmas Eve? Have a special dessert on your birthday? Watch fireworks on the Fourth of July?

Talk with your family about your favorite traditions. Share stories about the birthdays and holidays you remember most. Talk about the traditions that are most important to you.

As a family, think about the traditions you'd like to keep *and* dream about some new traditions you can create together.

Family Math Is Special

Do you like math? Maybe you are learning how to add and subtract numbers. Let's see: 2 + 2 + 3 = ___. 6 - 2 = ___. Did you get the right answers? Very good!

Family math is different. In family math, members can only be added to the family. No one is taken away. Even though someone might die or move away, they're still part of the family.

Here's a fun project to do: draw a picture of your whole family. Remember your family math!

When you add more members, you add more love!

ME

Cynthia Geisen has served as a chaplain, an advocate for survivors of domestic and sexual violence, and as a pastor of congregations that are in transition. She has written several books and booklets for Abbey Press Publications, including the children's books *We Are Alike, We Are Different: A Book About Diversity* and *What Is God Like?: A Book About God.*

R. W. Alley is the illustrator for the popular Abbey Press series of Elf-help books, as well as an illustrator and writer of children's books. He lives in Barrington, Rhode Island, with his wife, daughter, and son. See a wide variety of his works at: www.rwalley.com.